FREAK THE MIGHTY

by
Rodman Philbrick

Teacher Guide

Written by:
Jean Jamieson

> ## Note
> The Point Signature paperback edition of the book published by Scholastic Inc. was used to prepare this teacher guide. The page references may differ in the hardcover or other paperback editions.

ISBN 1-56137-900-X

To order, contact your local
school supply store, or—

Novel Units, Inc.
P.O. Box 791610
San Antonio, TX 78279

Table of Contents

Skills and Strategies

Thinking
Comparing, evaluating, analyzing
details, explaining opinions,
summarizing, organizing

Comprehension
Predicting, comparing, story
mapping, defining, sequencing,
describing

Literary Elements
Character analysis, setting, plot,
figurative language, literary
analysis, suspense, irony,
character motivation, point of
view, simile, rationalization

Listening/Speaking
Participation in discussions, role-
playing, participation in dramatic
activities, defending opinions,
describing, working with a partner

Writing
Research, short paragraphs,
captions, reports, poetry, written
statements, creative writing

Vocabulary
Target words, target word maps,
use and effectiveness of words,
synonyms, word comparisons,
sorting, root/base words

Summary of *Freak the Mighty*

Max Kane and Kevin Avery are reunited the summer before they enter eighth grade. The boys are opposites in physical appearance. Max's body is growing faster than usual, and Kevin's body is not growing much at all. For some reason, Max has been called slow, dumb and stupid most of his life. In contrast, Kevin is considered to be very intelligent. Max lives with his grandparents. Killer Kane, Max's father, is in prison for the murder of Max's mother. Kevin's father deserted Kevin and his mother when Kevin's birth defect became known. Max and Kevin become friends and join strengths to become Freak the Mighty, "slaying dragons and fools and walking high above the world." (page 40)

About the Author

Rodman Philbrick worked a variety of laboring jobs—longshoreman, carpenter, boat builder—while trying to make a living as a writer. At twenty-seven years of age, Philbrick decided that he would write suspense novels for adults. Within a short time he was able to give up the part-time jobs. Philbrick's mysteries, thrillers and detective stories enabled him to earn his living by his wits. It was an editor-friend who suggested that Philbrick write for young adults. *Freak the Mighty* came into fruition with Philbrick believing that the story had no commercial value. To the contrary, the story had a profound influence on his career as a writer. Although Philbrick has not given up writing adult novels, he has realized that he has stories to tell young readers.

Background Information

Morquio Syndrome :
Please check the synonyms listed below to find other names for this specific disorder.

Morquio Syndrome A
Galactosamine-6-Sulfatase Deficiency
Morquio-Brailsford Syndrome
Osteochondrodystrophy Deformans
Chondroosteodystrophy
Morquio Syndrome B
Beta-Galactosidase Deficiency Morquio Syndrome
Morquio Disease
MPS IV
Mucopolysaccharidosis IV

Mucopolysaccharidoses (MPS Disorders) are a group of rare genetic disorders caused by the deficiency of one of ten specific lysosomal enzymes, resulting in an inability to metabolize complex carbohydrates (mucopolysaccharides) into simpler molecules.

The accumulation of these large, undegraded mucopolysaccharides in the cells of the body causes a number of physical symptoms and abnormalities. Morquio Syndrome (MPS IV) exists in 2 forms: Morquio Syndromes A and B are due to a deficiency in the enzyme N-acetyl-galactosamine-6-sulfatase and beta-galactosidase, respectively. Deficiency of either enzyme leads to an accumulation of keratan sulfate and bony abnormalities of the head, chest, hands, knees and spine may occur as a result of this metabolic defect, with preservation of intellect. The skeletal abnormalities in MPS IV-B are usually milder that in MPS IV-A. Internet site, January, 1997—http://www.stepstn.com/nord/rdb_sum/299.htm

The "Bionic" Future of Medical Implants:

The search for replacement of natural body parts goes back to the ancient Egyptians who are known to have used dental implants. Today, growth in the use of medical implants is exponential. Surveys show that some 11 million Americans have at least one medical implant. These implants include: fixation devices used to assist healing of fractures, lens implants, artificial joints, heart pacemakers, and artificial heart valves. According to a recent report, medical device implants are expected to become one of the most promising areas of medicine in the next decade.

Nonetheless, many patients with medical device implants experience healing problems, defects or failure of the implant, infection, bleeding, or blood clots. New revolutions in biology, materials engineering, and computer science are making it possible to design and develop "bioactive" materials that are part natural, part synthetic. These materials will help to make medical implants of the 21st century more acceptable to the human body.

The Biomedical Engineering Center is combining expertise in molecular, cellular and structural biology, synthetic chemistry, cellular and tissue engineering, materials and interfacial science, and computer modeling to develop bioactive materials and artificial biomembranes for the medical implants of the 21st century. Interdisciplinary teams of scientists and engineers in the center's specialized laboratories are using new technologies to create biomaterials that mimic different tissues and organs such as skin, cornea, vessels, liver, and others that stimulate regeneration of nerves, remodeling of bone, and wound healing. Methods of extending the shelf life of cells and tissue replacements are being developed through cryobiology. Basic and applied research in biomaterials, cellular and tissue engineering, and nanotechnology are promising a "bionic" future. (Created 09/02/96 by Kevin G. Rau) Internet site, January, 1997—http://online.dct.com/~cyrkithra/corp002.txt

Robotics:

According to the Robot Institute of America, a robot is "a reprogrammable, multifunctional manipulator designed to move materials, parts, tools, or specialized devices through various programmed motions for the performance of a variety of tasks."

The word *robot* was coined by the Czech playwright Karel Capek from the Czech word for forced labor or serf. Capek was reportedly several times a candidate for the Nobel prize for his works, and was very influential and prolific as a writer and playwright. He died in 1938, before the Gestapo got to him for his anti-Nazi sympathies. The use of the word *robot* was introduced into his play *R.U.R. (Rossum's Universal Robots)* which opened in Prague in January of 1921. The play was an enormous success and productions soon opened throughout Europe and the US. *R.U.R's* theme, in part, was the dehumanization of man in a technological civilization.

The term *robotics* refers to the study and use of robots. The term was coined and first used by the Russian-born American scientist and writer Isaac Asimov. Asimov wrote prodigiously on a wide variety of subjects. He was best known for his many works of science fiction. The word *robotics* was first used in "Runaround," a short story published in 1942. *I, Robot*, a collection of several of these stories, was published in 1950.

The first industrial modern robots were the Unimates developed by George Devol and Joe Engelberger in the late 50's and early 60's. The first patents were by Devol for parts transfer machines. Engelberger formed Unimation and was the first to market robots. As a result, Engelberger has been called the "father of robotics." However, tele-operated or remote controlled devices had been built even earlier, with at least the first radio controlled vehicles built by Nikola Tesla in the 1890's. Modern industrial arms have increased in capability and performance through controller and language development, improved mechanisms, sensing, and drive systems. In the early to mid 80's the robot industry grew very fast primarily due to large investments by the automotive industry. (Robotics Internet Resource Page: This is a source of pointers to a wide variety of Robotics-related work on the Internet. This includes files, video, images, tele-operation etc. Use your favorite internet browser to check it out.)

Note:
It is not intended that everything presented in this guide be done. Please be selective, and use discretion when choosing the activities you will do with the unit. The choices that are made should be appropriate for your use and your group of students. A wide range of activities has been provided so that individuals as well as groups may benefit.

Introductory Information and Activities

Schedule Guest Speakers and Volunteers:
Some suggested topics and people of interest: robotics, bionic prosthesis use, parole officer, physically and mentally challenged students, professionals dealing with the physically and mentally challenged, professionals using bionic implants, etc.

Previewing the Book:
Look at the cover of the book. What has the cover artist chosen to tell about the story? At what time of the year do you think the story takes place? What do you think is the setting of the story? Two story characters are pictured. What do you think the ages of these characters might be? Read the words under the picture. Which character do you think is Max? Which character do you think is Freak?

Bulletin Board:
Form groups of students with similar interests to use bulletin boards to accompany the areas of study. For example:

A. Friendship
    1. Cover the bulletin board with background paper.
    2. Use the word *FRIENDSHIP* as the caption for the board.
    3. Place definitions of *friendship* on the board.

B. Robotics
    1. Define *ROBOTICS* and use as caption of the board.
    2. Make illustrations of some uses of *robotics* to place on the board.

C. Bionic Medical Implants
    1. Post defined terms on the board.
    2. Obtain or make illustrations of some current bionic medical implants.

D. Physically and Mentally Challenged Individuals
    1. List some causes and consequences.
    2. Define some terms used.

Prereading Activity:
Place the word TEAMWORK on a large sheet of paper. Ask the students to respond with words or ideas they think of when seeing this word. Record responses on the paper. For example: *cooperation, coordination, community, collaboration, unity, esprit de corps, common cause, alliance, fellowship, concert, collusion, unanimity, harmony,* etc.

Prereading Discussion:
Discuss the advantages and disadvantages of working with others. Record on paper. Is teamwork more advantageous at certain times?

Personal Observations:

Have students keep personal journals to record their feelings and comments as the situations in *Freak the Mighty* are discussed. They also might want to write about how they think they might handle similar situations, such as: being raised by grandparents, being large or small in size as compared to peers, having difficulty reading, being friendless, etc. These journals do not have to be shared.

Recommended Book List:

Display a large sheet of paper in the room. Ask students to fill in the requested information, to share books they would recommend to others.

Book Title	Author	Comments

Vocabulary Activities

What is the Target Word?
Have the students act out some of the vocabulary words. Find out if classmates can guess the target words. Some suggested words for *Freak the Mighty*, Chapters 1-4, might include: glimpse 7, hunkering 8, scuttle 10, huffed 12, flimsy 12, and robotics 18.

Target Word Map:
Complete the following word map for target words from *Freak the Mighty*. Suggestions include: intruding 22, offended 23, trajectory 34, nanosecond 36, evasive 43, and confrontation 43, from Chapters 5-8.

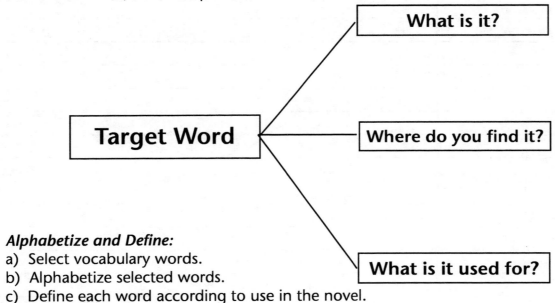

Alphabetize and Define:
a) Select vocabulary words.
b) Alphabetize selected words.
c) Define each word according to use in the novel.

Use in a Sentence:
a) Select a group of vocabulary words.
b) Use as many of the words as possible in one sentence.

Word Comparison:
a) Choose two vocabulary words and explain how they go together.

_____ and _____ go together because

_____ .

b) Choose two vocabulary words and explain why they do not go together.

_____ and _____ are not usually related because

_____ .

Synonym Match:
a) Select vocabulary words from a chapter under study.
b) List one synonym for each vocabulary word on a small piece of paper.
c) Mix the pieces of paper.
d) Match each synonym to the appropriate vocabulary word.

Root/Base Words:
Find the base or root word for at least eight vocabulary words. Look at each word. What is the meaning of the root word? What is the meaning of the vocabulary word? What prefix or suffix has been added to the vocabulary word? How has the meaning of the root word changed by the addition? Some suggested vocabulary words: unvanquished 1, microsecond 6, mainstream 6, humanoid 10, ornithopter 13, etc.

Vocabulary Sort:
Classify a group of vocabulary words into names of things (nouns), action words (verbs), and describing words (adjectives and adverbs).

Odd One Out:
Use vocabulary words from one or two chapters. Make a chain of four words. One word of the chain is the vocabulary word, two words are synonyms of the vocabulary word, and one word does not go with the others. (Mix the sequence of the words in the chain.) Underline the word that does not belong with the others. Explain why it does not belong.

Word Use and Effectiveness:
a) Select vocabulary words.
b) Group words by use.
c) Create a synonym train for each word.
d) Substitute a synonym for the vocabulary word in a sentence.
e) Compare the effectiveness of the thought conveyed in that sentence.

Recommended Procedure:
It is recommended that the book be read two chapters at a time, but combining the last three. As each pair ends, predictions may be made as to what might happen next. These predictions are, in reality, good guesses based upon what has already happened in the story and on the clues given by the author. Predictions may be reviewed as the story continues. Knowledge of vocabulary words may be reviewed either individually or as a group by having students write or give simple definitions. These definitions may then be checked by seeing how the words are used in context as the story is read. If any definition is unclear, a dictionary may be used.

Using Predictions in the Novel Unit Approach

We all make predictions as we read—little guesses about what will happen next, how the conflict will be resolved, which details given by the author will be important to the plot, which details will help to fill in our sense of a character. Students should be encouraged to predict, to make sensible guesses. As students work on predictions, these discussion questions can be used to guide them: What are some of the ways to predict? What is the process of a sophisticated reader's thinking and predicting? What clues does an author give us to help us in making our predictions? Why are some predictions more likely than others?

A predicting chart is for students to record their predictions. As each subsequent chapter is discussed, you can review and correct previous predictions. This procedure serves to focus on predictions and to review the stories.

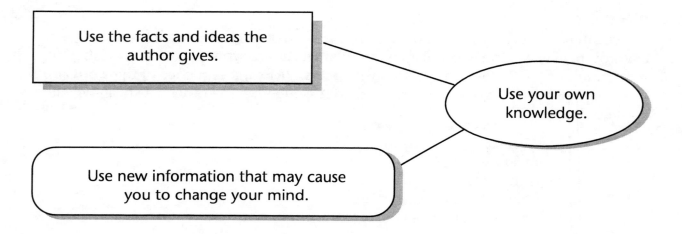

Prediction Chart

What characters have we met so far?	What is the conflict in the story?	What are your predictions?	Why did you make those predictions?

Story Map

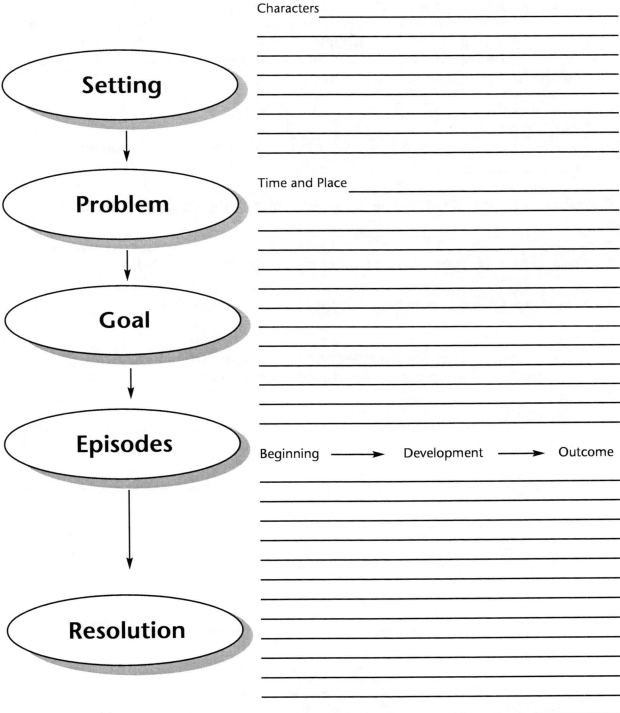

Setting

Problem

Goal

Episodes

Resolution

Characters _____

_____

_____

_____

_____

_____

_____

Time and Place _____

_____

_____

_____

_____

_____

_____

_____

_____

Beginning ⟶ Development ⟶ Outcome

_____

_____

_____

_____

_____

_____

_____

_____

_____

_____

Using Character Webs—In the Novel Unit Approach

Attribute Webs are simply a visual representation of a character from the novel. They provide a systematic way for the students to organize and recap the information they have about a particular character. Attribute webs may be used after reading the novel to recapitulate information about a particular character or completed gradually as information unfolds, done individually, or finished as a group project.

One type of character attribute web uses these divisions:

- How a character acts and feels. (How does the character feel in this picture? How would you feel if this happened to you? How do you think the character feels?)

- How a character looks. (Close your eyes and picture the character. Describe him to me.)

- Where a character lives. (Where and when does the character live?)

- How others feel about the character. (How does another specific character feel about our character?)

In group discussion about the student attribute webs and specific characters, the teacher can ask for backup proof from the novel. You can also include inferential thinking.

Attribute webs need not be confined to characters. They may also be used to organize information about a concept, object or place.

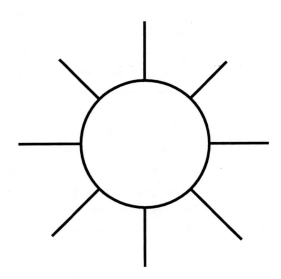

Chapter-by-Chapter Vocabulary, Discussion Questions, and Activities

Chapter 1: "The Unvanquished Truth"—Pages 1-4
Chapter 2: "Up from the Down Under"—Pages 5-9

Summary:

Max Kane is the narrator of the story. It is the summer before Max enters eighth grade, the summer that he grows so fast. Max starts by recalling the times he has seen the person who eventually joins him to become "Freak the Mighty." Kevin and his mother, Gwen, move into the duplex down the way from Max's grandparents' home on the first of July. Kevin does not look like he has grown any since last seen by Max when in third grade.

Vocabulary:

unvanquished 1	phony 2	laser 3	duplex 4
observation 5	microsecond 6	mainstream 6	glimpse 7
hunkering 8	consequences 8		

Discussion Questions:

1. Who is telling the story? *(Pages 1-3, The story is being told by Max, who was given the nickname of "Kicker" when in day care.)*

2. Why is Max given the nickname of Kicker while in day care? *(Pages 1-2, Max does not want to be hugged or touched, so he kicks anyone who touches him.)*

3. Why do you think Max feels that "hug stuff" is a "rotten lie"? *(page 2, opinion)*

4. When has Max previously seen the person who later pairs up with him to become "Freak the Mighty"? *(Pages 1-3, Max has seen this boy when in day care and again when in third grade.)* What attributes does this boy have that makes it easy for Max to remember him? *(Page 2, The boy is small in stature, uses crutches, and has leg braces. In day care, the boy calls himself "Robot Man.")*

5. What opinion do you think Max has of himself as the story begins? Why do you think he feels this way? *(opinion)*

6. With whom does Max live? *(Page 1, Max lives with his grandparents, the parents of his mother.)* Why? *(Page 3, Max's mother is dead.)*

7. What happens on the first day of July in Max's neighborhood? *(Pages 6-9, Gwen and Kevin move into a duplex down the block from Max's grandparents' home. Kevin is "Robot Man" from day care.)*

8. What is Max's impression of Kevin after their first encounter in front of the duplex? *(Page 9, Max thinks, "He wants me to die.")* Why do you think Max feels this way? *(opinion)*

Supplementary Activities:

1. Literary Analysis—Character's Motivation: A character's actions often tell the reader something about the character's thoughts and feelings. What do you think Kevin's motives might be for his treatment of Max as Kevin moves into the neighborhood? (pages 8-9)

2. Start character attribute webs for Max and Kevin. Add to the webs as more is learned about them. (Characterization is the way an author lets the reader know what the characters are like. In direct characterization, the author describes the character directly. In indirect characterization, the author provides clues about the character through thoughts, speech and actions.)

3. You know Max's feelings about hugs. What are yours? Give your opinion in quatrain poetry form. A quatrain poem is written in four lines. It may be rhymed or unrhymed. If rhymed, the pattern used is the decision of the author.

4. Make an illustration to go with the term "Robot Man."

5. Describe the kind of look you think Kevin gives Max that relays the feeling of hate to Max. (pages 8-9)

Chapter 3: "American Flyer"—Pages 10-14
Chapter 4: "What Frightened the Fair Gwen"—Pages 15-20

Summary:
Later that day, Kevin's ornithopter gets stuck a in backyard tree. Even standing in a wagon and hitting at it with a crutch does not dislodge the mechanical bird. Seeing this, Max goes over to get the bird down for Kevin. Pulling Kevin in his wagon, Max takes him to see the "down under." While there, Kevin tells Max about King Arthur and the Knights of the Round Table. Gwen searches for Kevin and quickly takes her son home after seeing Max.

Vocabulary:

scuttle 10	humanoid 10	bulkhead 11	huffed 12
flimsy 12	ornithopter 13	installation 13	propulsion 13
replacement 13	sobriquet 15	demeanor 15	postulated 16
quest 17	invincible 17	limitations 18	robotics 18
sophisticated 18	opiate 19	massives 19	

Discussion Questions:

1. Why does Max go over to Kevin's backyard? *(Page 12, Kevin cannot get something down out of the tree. Max goes over to take it down for Kevin.)* What is it? *(Page 13, It is an ornithopter, a mechanical bird.)*

2. What do the boys do after the bird is rescued? *(Page 13, They play with it. Kevin activates the bird, and Max retrieves it.)* Why do they stop? *(Page 13, The elastic breaks.)*

3. Why does Max take Kevin over to see the "down under"? *(Page 14, Max thinks it's easier to show Kevin than to explain the "down under" to him.)*

4. Why does Kevin call his mother "Fair Gwen of Air"? *(Page 16, Kevin's mother's name is Gwen. He sometimes calls her Fair Guinevere, from the legend of King Arthur. Max thinks the name sounds like "Fair Gwen of Air.")*

5. Why is Kevin so interested in King Arthur and the Knights of the Round Table? *(Pages 17-18, Because the knights wore armor, Kevin thinks they "were like the first human version of robots." Kevin goes on to tell Max, "It's pretty amazing, really, that hundreds of years before they had computers they were already attempting to exceed the design limitations of the human body.")* What do you think some purposes of the armor might be?

6. What is Max thinking as Gwen takes Kevin home? *(Page 20, Max thinks that Gwen is afraid of him.)* What would make Max think that? What about Max might frighten Gwen?

Supplementary Activities:

1. Literary Analysis—Foreshadowing: Foreshadowing is indicating or suggesting an event beforehand. Foreshadowing provides a hint of what is to occur later. What do you think might be indicated by what is presented about Kevin's health? "…and he sounds like he can hardly breathe." (page 12) "He's able to hump down the steps by himself, except it makes him sort of out of breath, you can hear him wheezing or I guess you'd call it panting, like a dog does on a hot day." (page 15)

2. Write a description of a room that you use frequently. Have someone who is also familiar with the room read the description. Is that person able to identify the room?

3. Kevin refers to the legend of King Arthur in Chapter 4. Go to the library. Read something about King Arthur. What do you think of him? Write a note to Kevin expressing your opinion of the king.

Chapter 5: "Spitting Image"—Pages 21-27
Chapter 6: "Close Encounter of the Turd Kind"—Pages 28-33

Summary:

Gwen invites Max over for supper, and he has a great time. He goes home happy. On the Fourth of July, Max and Kevin are allowed to go to view the fireworks together at the millpond. On the way, the boys are stopped by Tony D. and his punksters. The sound of a siren and the appearance of a police car chase the punksters away. So he can see the fireworks at the millpond, Max sets Kevin on his shoulders.

Vocabulary:

intruding 22	impression 23	offended 23	spastic 25
flinch 26	depleted 26	expel 27	regurgitate 27
cretin 31	punksters 31		

Discussion Questions:

1. What is Max's *time out*? *(Page 21, It is a place inside his head. Max describes it as being cool and empty. "You're nothing, you're nobody, nothing matters, you're not even there.")* Where in his room does Max go in order to get to his *time out*? *(Page 21, Max lies on the floor under his bed because it is very dark there.)*

2. Why does Gram come to Max's room? *(Pages 22-23, Gram comes with a message for Max from Gwen Avery. Gwen called to apologize and to invite Max over for supper.)*

3. How does Max reply to Gram's calling Kevin a "poor boy"? *(Page 24, Max disagrees with Gram, saying, "He's not a poor boy. You should hear him talk. I think the rest of him is so small because his brain is so big.")*

4. What is it about Max that startles Gwen when she first sees him? *(Page 25, Max is the "spitting image" of his father.)*

5. Why does Max feel that everyone thinks it's a "big deal" that he looks like his father? *(Page 26, Max feels that way because his father is in prison.)* How do you think others would feel about the resemblance of Max and his father if things were different?

6. Do Max, Kevin and Gwen enjoy their time together? *(Pages 26-27, Yes. They laugh a lot, enjoy good food and enjoy one another's company. Max goes home happy.)*

7. Why is this Fourth of July special for Max? *(Page 29, This is the first year Max gets to go to see the fireworks without Grim and Gram. Max and Kevin are allowed to go together.)*

8. What happens to the boys on the way to the millpond? *(Pages 29-30, Max and Kevin are stopped by Tony D. and his punksters.)* Why do the punksters leave? *(Page 31, A police car drives by with its siren going.)*

9. Why does Max put Kevin on his shoulders? *(Page 32, Max puts Kevin on his shoulders so that Kevin can see the fireworks.)* How does Kevin react to this? *(Pages 32-33, Kevin is delighted.)*

Supplementary Activities:

1. Literary Analysis—Facts and Opinions: Facts are statements that one can prove. Opinions are statements that tell what someone thinks about something. Find some facts and opinions expressed in Chapter 5. Write at least two examples of each on a sheet of paper. Discuss examples with a partner. What might happen if an opinion is not based on a fact?

2. What is pyrotechnics? Do some research. Find out about it. Share your information with others. Can you locate a pyrotechnist to interview?

3. Using the art media of your choice, create something that represents a burst of fireworks to you. Give your work a title and place it on display.

4. On page 22, Gram is talking to Max. Gram mentions that Kevin and Max seem to be "making friends." Max thinks that is a "wet idea." What do you think Max means by that? What is something different that might be substituted for that term? Write your answers on a sheet of paper.

Chapter 7: "Walking High Above the World"—Pages 34-40
Chapter 8: "Dinosaur Brain"—Pages 41-47

Summary:
On their way to the food carts after the fireworks, with Kevin still on Max's shoulders, Max and Kevin are accosted by Tony D. and his punks. Kevin steers Max to the millpond, where they are able to distance themselves from their attackers. Kevin alerts a roving police car, and Max becomes somewhat of a hero. When asked for identification by the police, Kevin tells them that they are "Freak the Mighty." Grim and Gram are impressed by Max's heroics. Kevin changes Max's daily summer routine by coming over to wake Max every morning with an idea of a quest for Freak the Mighty.

Vocabulary:

perspective 34	trajectory 34	nanosecond 36	megaphone 39
possessed 42	evasive 43	confrontation 43	clunker 44
vegetate 44	archetype 45		

Discussion Questions:

1. When Kevin is on Max's shoulders, do both boys see the same things? *(Page 34, No. Max reminds Kevin that he is up an additional two feet.)* Does this come in handy? *(Pages 34-37, Yes. Kevin is able to spot Tony D. and his punksters and then direct Max away from them.)*

2. Where do the boys have to go to get away from their pursuers? *(Page 37, Max has to wade into the pond. The mud sucks up to and then beyond his knees.)* What happens to Tony D. as he follows Max into the pond? *(Page 37, Not being as tall as Max, Tony soon has just his head above water. His punksters have to rescue him.)* Do you think this would mollify or anger Tony D.? Why?

3. How do Max and Kevin get out of the pond? *(Pages 38-39, Kevin sees a cruising police car and whistles it down. The police use ropes to pull Max and Kevin out.)*

4. When asked for their names, what does Kevin reply? *(Pages 39-40, "We're Freak the Mighty, that's who we are." The extra-tall combo is known as Freak the Mighty from then on.)*

5. How do Grim and Gram react to Max's pond adventure? *(Pages 41-42, They treat Max like a hero and are proud of him.)* Do you think this will change Max's life any?

6. How does Kevin change Max's summer routine? *(Pages 44-45, Kevin comes over every morning to wake Max and to prepare him for the day's quest.)*

7. While Max provides the foot-power for Freak the Mighty, what does Kevin provide? *(opinion)*

Supplementary Activities:

1. Literary Analysis—Irony: An ironic situation is one that turns out quite differently from what one expects. When a narrator or character makes an ironic comment, he recognizes a contrast between appearance and reality, or between what is expected and what really happens. At the bottom of page 41, Max makes the comment, "Me rescuing Freak. What a joke, right?" Do you think he feels that to be an ironic assessment of the situation? Why or why not? Write an explanation of the situation and give your assessment.

2. Make an attribute web for Tony D. Write an explanation as to why you think he acts as he does.

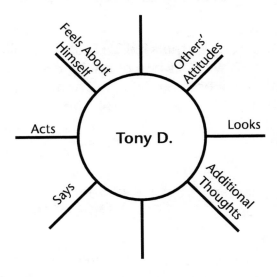

3. If Freak the Mighty were to ask you to choose a location for a quest in your area, what would you recommend? Why?

Name of Quest Location:

_____

Reasons for Recommendation: _____

_____

How to get to location from:

_____

_____

_____

What to look for at location:

_____

_____

_____

Notes: _____

_____

Chapter 9: "Life Is Dangerous"—Pages 48-53
Chapter 10: "Rats or Worse"—Pages 54-62

Summary:
Freak the Mighty goes on a quest to the Medical Research building at the hospital. Max is sworn to secrecy, and Kevin tells him of the bionic research effort being made to develop a human robot that will be his new body. Another quest requires the boys to go out at three in the morning to retrieve a purse from a storm drain. An ID card has a lady's name on it—Loretta Lee.

Vocabulary:

artifact 49	avarice 49	yonder 49	incision 51
divulged 51	bionic 51	modification 51	smug 54
teleportation 55	optimum 56	retrieval 60	damsel 62

Discussion Questions:

1. What does Freak reply when Max asks, "How do you know which way is East?" *(Page 49, Freak shows Max a compass.)* How does a directional compass work? See Supplementary Activities #2.

2. What is the destination of Freak the Mighty in Chapter 9? *(Page 50, The destination is a part of the local hospital, the new Medical Research building.)* Why? *(Pages 51-52, Freak tells Max, who is sworn to secrecy, that a whole new body is being developed for him in the Experimental Bionics Unit.)*

3. Does Max believe Freak's explanation? *(Page 52, Max thinks, "I can tell he really means it.")*

4. What does Max understand about this quest? *(Page 52, "This is why we came here, so Freak could show me where he's been. The place is important to him. I understand this much, even if I still don't understand about bionics or what it means to be a human robot.")* Do you think Kevin will share this place only with Max, or will he share it with others? Why do you think as you do?

5. What is the purpose of the next quest for Freak the Mighty? *(Page 55, The next quest is a treasure hunt, without the "hunt.")* Why don't the boys have to hunt? *(Pages 55-56, Freak already knows where the treasure is. He tells Max, "The treasure is hidden in a storm drain.")*

6. In what way is this quest to be different from others? *(Page 56, This quest is to take place at three in the morning, with Freak the Mighty wearing black.)*

7. What does Freak the Mighty retrieve from the storm drain? *(Pages 61-62, The treasure is a purse belonging to Loretta Lee.)* What would you do with something you have found? Why?

Supplementary Activities:
1. Literary Analysis—Amplification: *Amplification* is comprised of the particulars by which a statement is expanded, made larger or greater in importance or intensity. Find a statement or incident in Chapter 9 that is an example of amplification. Copy your choice on a sheet of paper. Give the page number on which it appears. Tell why you think this is an example of amplification.

2. Freak sometimes makes things up as the boys are going on their quest. An ordinary sidewalk may become a dangerous bridge. (page 48) Write a short story in which a sidewalk changes into something else. What adventure does this lead to? Tell all about it.

3. Do some research. Find out more about the directional compass.

4. Freak has names for the homes in the ritzy neighborhood. (page 49) Choose a local neighborhood. Write a description of that neighborhood and create names for at least three man-made structures in that neighborhood. Make an illustration to go with your written description.

5. Freak defines *pain* as "a state of mind." (page 53) Write out your own definition of *pain*, and make a list of everything that comes to your mind that relates to *pain*.

Chapter 11: "The Damsel of Distress"—Pages 63-71
Chapter 12: "Killer Kane, Killer Kane, Had a Kid Who Got No Brain"— Pages 72-79

Summary:
Freak the Mighty goes to the New Testaments to return the purse to Loretta Lee. Loretta is married to Iggy Lee, boss of The Panheads, a motorcycle gang. Loretta and Iggy know Killer Kane. The boys are frightened, but are not harmed. At school, Gwen arranges it so that Max is placed in Kevin's classes.

Vocabulary:

oaths 64	reconsider 64	fidgety 64	hombre 70

Discussion Questions:
1. What does Kevin explain to Max about quests and a promise? *(Page 63, "Freak explains how it's okay to break a promise if you're on a quest.")* Do you agree or disagree with Kevin? Why?

2. What do Kevin and Max each gain by being Freak the Mighty? *(Page 64, Kevin does not have to wear his leg brace or carry his crutches. Max likes "how it feels to have a really smart brain" on his shoulders, helping him think.)* What are some additional pluses for the two boys?

3. Who does Freak the Mighty meet when returning the purse? *(Pages 65-66, Loretta and Iggy Lee are at the address listed on the ID in the purse.)* Who is Iggy Lee? *(Page 66, Iggy Lee is boss of The Panheads, a motorcycle gang.)*

4. Why is Freak the Mighty allowed to leave the Lees' apartment without being harmed? *(Page 70, Max is recognized as the son of Killer Kane.)*

5. Why is Max allowed to be in the same classes with Kevin? *(Page 75, "He [Kevin] made the Fair Gwen go in and see all these people at the school, because I [Max] wasn't supposed to be in the smart classes, no way, and finally they all agreed it would be good for Freak, having someone to help him get around.")* How do you think Kevin could get around school without Max?

6. How does Kevin restore order in English class on the first day of school? *(Page 77, Kevin climbs up on his desk and calls for order.)* Why do you think this works?

7. What does Kevin do to show Mrs. Donelli how he is sometimes *more* than Kevin? *(Pages 77-78, Kevin and Max show Mrs. Donelli Freak the Mighty.)*

Supplementary Activities:
1. Literary Analysis—Simile: Similes are comparisons using such words as: *like, as, than, similar to, resembles*, etc. to highlight comparisons. The author uses a simile on the bottom of page 76 to compare the look the English teacher, Mrs. Donelli, has on her face to a different look. What is it? Find additional similes in Chapters 11 and 12. Copy the similes on a sheet of paper and tell what is being compared.

2. Couplets are two-line poems that match in length and rhyme. Create a couplet for Freak the Mighty. For example:　　　　*After returning from a quest*
　　　　Freak the Mighty likes to rest.

Chapter 13: "American Chop Suey"—Pages 80-87
Chapter 14: "Cross My Heart and Hope to Die"—Pages 88-92

Summary:

It's October and Friday the Thirteenth. Max is called into Mrs. Addison's office to be told that his father would like to see him. Max gets hysterical and Mrs. Addison promises to prevent any contact by Killer Kane. At lunch, Kevin chokes on the American chop suey and is taken to the hospital in an ambulance. Kevin comes home the next day, and all goes well for Freak the Mighty until Christmas vacation. Max learns that his father is up for parole and promises Grim that he will stay in the house. Grim has a court order preventing Kenny Kane from coming within a mile of the house.

Vocabulary:

dyslexic 81	detention 84	gruel 86	biogenic 88
expression 89	ruckus 91		

Discussion Questions:

1. By October, how are things going at school for Kevin and Max? *(Page 80, Things are going well for both boys, and they are being accepted as a unit.)*

2. What is the opinion of Max's reading skills tutor? *(Page 81, Mr. Meehan tells Max that "hanging out with Kevin" has improved Max's skills and attitude.)* What does Kevin do to help Max? *(Page 81, Kevin has been showing Max how to read a whole book in a way that makes sense to Max. Page 82, "The reading stuff Freak helped me figure out by showing how words are just voices on paper.")*

3. How is Max doing with his writing? *(Page 82, "Writing down the words is a whole different story. No matter what Freak says, writing the stuff down is not like talking...")* To what would you compare writing?

4. What happens first on Friday the Thirteenth in October? *(Pages 82-85, Max is called to the principal's office and is told that his father would like to see him. Max gets hysterical. Mrs. Addison promises Max he will not have to do anything he doesn't want to do.)* Why do you think Max gets so upset? Do you think Mrs. Addison will be able to keep her promise? Why or why not?

5. What happens in the cafeteria at lunch on the thirteenth? *(Pages 86-87, Kevin chokes on his lunch. Max gets the school nurse, who has someone call an ambulance. Kevin is taken to the hospital.)*

6. When is the next upset in Max's life? *(Pages 89-91, The next upset occurs during Christmas vacation. Max learns that his father is up for parole.)* What has Grim already done to help Max? *(Page 91, Grim tells Max, "What I did do, just so you know, I went into court and made it so he won't be allowed within a mile of this house. If he does try to come here, they'll send him back to prison, the judge promised me that much.")* Do you think a court order will keep Killer Kane away from Max? Why or why not?

7. What does Max promise Grim? *(Page 92, Max promises Grim that he will stay in the house.)* Do you think Max's promise will affect Kevin? Why or why not? If so, how?

Supplementary Activities:
1. Literary Analysis—Point of View: Writers can tell their stories from many points of view. Sometimes a central character in the story tells the story. Sometimes the story teller is a minor character. Sometimes the story teller is a narrator who can see inside the characters and sometimes the writer shifts the point of view from one person to another. Who tells most of the story of Freak the Mighty? Write an episode in which a different character tells the story. How does the point of view change?

2. Invite a police officer, a judge, or an attorney to explain parole and the court order to the group.

3. Given a choice, would you rather read a story or write a story? Why? Do one or the other. Those who write the stories may have them read by the readers.

4. Use a Venn diagram to compare Max and Kevin. How are they alike? How are they different?

Kevin   Both   Max

Chapter 15: "What Came Down the Chimney"—Pages 93-99
Chapter 16: "A Chip off the Old Block"—Pages 100-107

Summary:
It's Christmas Eve. Gwen and Kevin join Max, Gram and Grim for supper and an exchange of gifts. Kevin has made Max a dictionary of his favorite words with his special definitions. Later that night, Killer Kane comes to take Max away. Their first stop is the apartment of Loretta and Iggy Lee.

Vocabulary:

specialties 94   gizmo 95   pyramid 96   deprived 103

Discussion Questions:

1. How does Grim differentiate between lies and tales? *(Page 95, Grim tells Gram, "Lies are mean things, and tales are meant to entertain.")* Do you think it is obvious that Grim is telling a tale and not a lie about the stockings? Elaborate.

2. What is the shape of the box that Kevin has made for Max's gift? *(Page 96, Kevin has made a pyramid.)* What is special about it? *(Page 97, It is rigged so that all of the sides unfold at the same time.)*

3. What gift has Kevin made for Max? *(Page 97, Kevin has made Max a book of his favorite words. They are in alphabetical order, each word having Kevin's special definition.)*

4. What happens during the night while Grim, Gram and Max are sleeping? *(Pages 98-101, Killer Kane returns to get Max.)*

5. Is Max surprised to see his father? *(Page 101, "…none of this is a surprise. Somehow I always knew this would happen, that he would come for me, in the night, that I would wake up to find him there, filling the room, and that I'd feel empty.")*

6. Where does Killer Kane take Max? *(Page 105, Killer Kane takes Max to the apartment of Iggy and Loretta Lee.)* Do you think they are expected? Explain.

7. Are the Kanes going to stay with the Lees? *(Page 107, Iggy tells Killer Kane, "Any time you want, I'll show you that place I told you about.")* What can be surmised from this statement by Iggy?

Supplementary Activities:

1. Literary Analysis—Suspense: Suspense is a state of mental uncertainty, excitement, or indecision. In literature, suspense is a quality of tension in a plot which sustains interest and makes readers want to know what will happen next. How do you feel at the end of Chapter 15? What has the author interjected? How do you think will this change the story?

2. Make a list of six words you would like to add to Freak's dictionary. Define each word in your own unique way.

Chapter 17: "By All That's Holy"—Pages 108-114
Chapter 18: "Never Trust a Cripple"—Pages 115-121

Summary:

Iggy takes Killer Kane and Max to a vacant apartment in the New Testaments and leaves them there. Max is tied up by his father, who attaches the end of the rope to his own waist. Killer Kane explains to Max that he is now a preacher, and that they will be traveling to tell of Killer Kane's redemption. His father also swears to Max that he did not kill Max's mother. Flashing blue lights on Christmas morning warn the Kanes of police presence. Iggy arrives and blames the police inquiry on Kevin. Iggy promises to obtain transportation and a gun for Killer Kane.

Vocabulary:

dysfunctional 109   redeemed 118   illiterate 118   precaution 118
functional 121

Discussion Questions:

1. Where do Max and his father stay on Christmas Eve? *(Page 108, Iggy has located an apartment in the New Testaments that is vacant during the holiday. Iggy takes Killer Kane and Max there.)*

2. How is Max treated by his father? *(Page 110, Max's hands and feet are tied by Killer Kane, who then loops the end of the rope around his own waist.)* What does this treatment of Max indicate to you about Killer Kane? Explain.

3. Why does Killer Kane wake Max before daybreak? *(Page 111, Killer Kane tells Max, "First thing, like I already said, I never killed anybody. I'm big like you're big, so folks assume things they shouldn't." ... "As if a man should be blamed for how fearsome or cruel he looks, when in fact he's truly a loving person inside.")* Do you think Max believes his father? Why or why not? Do you agree or disagree with the premise that someone can be blamed for something because of appearance? Why?

4. What does Max notice as he looks at his father's face and listens to him speak of injustices he has experienced? *(Page 112, Max notices tears on his father's cheeks.)* What does Max notice about his father's voice? *(Pages 112-113, "There's no crying in his voice, you can't hear it there...")* How would you assess this situation?

5. What are Killer Kane's plans for the future? *(Pages 117-118, Killer Kane plans to take Max to a warmer climate in an RV bus. Max will collect money in a basket while his father tells people how he has redeemed himself.)* If Max had a choice, do you think he would want to do this? Why or why not?

6. When Iggy comes to the apartment, what does he report to Killer Kane? *(Pages 119-120, Iggy reports that he has had a visit from the police. They are looking for Max. Iggy says that Loretta saw Kevin in the police car.)*

7. What does Killer Kane need from Iggy? *(Page 121, He needs a firearm and a means of transportation.)* What do you think Killer Kane would do if he did not have help from Iggy?

Supplementary Activities:

1. Literary Analysis—Rationalization: Rationalization provides plausible but untrue reasons for conduct. On page 111, Killer Kane tells Max, "I'm big like you're big, so folks assume things they shouldn't." What are some of the things Killer Kane is attributing to his size? Does his rationalization seem reasonable? Do you think he is telling the truth? Why or why not? Explain.

2. On page 115, Max relates, "Looking down at him [Killer Kane] on the floor, how he overflows the rug, I think about that story where a giant falls asleep and is tied up by little people." To what story does Max refer? *(Gulliver's Travels by Jonathan Swift)* What story comes to your mind when you think of giants? What does that story bring to mind? Make a chain of at least six stories beyond Max's story.

   - *Freak the Mighty* by Rodman Philbrick
   - *Gulliver's Travels* by Jonathan Swift
   1. *James and the Giant Peach* by Roald Dahl
   2. *Alice's Adventures In Wonderland* by Lewis Carroll
   3. *Twenty Thousand Leagues Under the Sea* by Jules Verne
   4. *Around the World in Eighty Days* by Jules Verne
   5. *The Red Balloon* by Albert Lamorisse
   6. *The Big Yellow Balloon* by Edward Fenton

3. Max's father tells him, "Killer Kane, that's just an unkind nickname they hung on me." (page 112) Make a list of nicknames that you have heard. Are most of them unkind or kind? Why do you think that is? Change the nicknames so that all of them are kind. Make a list of five characters from this story. Give each character a kind nickname.

4. Make a prediction as to what you think will happen next in the story.

Chapter 19: "Into the Black Down Under"—Pages 122-127
Chapter 20: "Freak the Mighty Strikes Again"—Pages 128-134

Summary:

Killer Kane takes Max to a burned-out building on the other side of the alley. They hide in the basement. Max is bound and gagged by his father, who goes back upstairs to look around. Loretta sneaks downstairs and releases Max. Just as she finishes, Killer Kane returns and starts to strangle her. As Max tries to help, he remembers the murder of his mother and accuses his father. Killer Kane turns on Max, and Kevin comes in through a window, creating a diversion. Max grabs Kevin, gets up the stairs and bursts out of the boarded-up building. The police are there.

Vocabulary:

puny 123   slagged 125

Discussion Questions:

1. Why do Max and his father leave the apartment? *(Page 122, They leave as a precautionary measure, in case the police go door-to-door searching for Max.)* Where do they go? *(Page 122, Killer Kane takes Max to a burned-out building across the alley. They hide in the basement.)*

2. Does Killer Kane trust Max? How do you know? *(Page 124, Killer Kane tells Max, "Understand you can't be trusted quite yet." He gags Max and binds his hands and feet, tying Max's feet to an old boiler.)* Do you think all of Killer Kane's actions are necessary? Why or why not?

3. After Killer Kane goes upstairs to look around, who comes downstairs to help Max? *(Pages 125-126, Loretta Lee comes downstairs to help Max.)* Are you surprised at this turn of events? Explain.

4. What does Loretta whisper to Max as she tries to untie the rope's knots? *(Page 126, "Keeping your own kid tied up, it ain't right. He ain't the man I thought I remembered, that's for sure.")* Do you think Killer Kane has changed or that Loretta's memory of him has changed? Elaborate.

5. Does Loretta free Max? *(Pages 126-127, Yes, Max is freed.)* What happens next? *(Page 127, Killer Kane returns and starts to strangle Loretta.)* How do you think Killer Kane gets down the stairs without being heard by Loretta and/or Max?

6. What causes Killer Kane to shift his attention from Loretta to Max? *(Pages 128-129, Max remembers what he saw when he was four years old. Max tells Killer Kane, "I saw you kill her! I saw you kill Mom!")*

7. How does Kevin come to Max's rescue? *(Pages 131-133, Kevin breaks a window, comes in and squirts Killer Kane in the eyes with what he says is sulfuric acid. Max picks up Kevin and gets up the stairs and out of the building, with Killer Kane in pursuit. The police are waiting outside.)*

8. What is really in the squirt gun? *(Pages 133, Kevin has a mixture of soap, vinegar and curry powder.)* Do you think any one of the ingredients would have been effective alone? Why or why not?

9. What is happening to Max, Kevin, Loretta and Killer Kane as Chapter 20 ends? *(Pages 133-134, Max is being hugged by Gram, Kevin is being hugged by Gwen, Loretta is alive and being brought out of the cellar by the police, and Killer Kane is in handcuffs and shoved into the back of a police van.)* Did you predict any or all of these events?

Supplementary Activities:
1. Literary Analysis—Cliffhanger: A cliffhanger is a device used, often at the end of a chapter, to increase suspense. The reader is "left hanging"—eager to read on and to find out how a situation will be resolved or to find out what a mysterious statement means.

    What is the cliffhanger in Chapter 19? Make a list of different ways in which this situation might be resolved. Discuss your resolutions with other class members. As the story continues, find out if anyone came up with the same resolution used by the author.

2. Where do you think the other story characters are while Killer Kane is trying to strangle Loretta and Max? What do you think they might be doing? Dramatize different scenarios.

Chapter 21: "The Accident of Nature"—Pages 135-140
Chapter 22: "Remembering Is Just an Invention of the Mind"— Pages 141-146

Summary:
Killer Kane makes a deal and pleads guilty, so Max does not have to testify against his father. Spring arrives and school gets out. Two days later, it is Kevin's thirteenth birthday. Kevin's present is a new computer with a modem, in case he has to stay home from school he can go to school over the telephone. After Kevin's birthday dinner, Max helps in the kitchen while Kevin shows Grim how to play 3-D chess. Grim's shout of Kevin's name shatters the air. Kevin is having a seizure.

Vocabulary:
aberration 137	linear 143	accelerator 143
obnoxious 143	prodigy 143	

Discussion Questions:

1. What is the extent of Loretta's injury? *(Page 136, "The word is she's hurt pretty bad because he [Killer Kane] cracked a bone in her neck, but she'll be okay in the long run.")*

2. What is Max's opinion of Iggy at this time? *(Page 136, "Iggy, when I saw him that time in the hospital waiting, he was chewing a hole right through his beard he was so worried, and it made me think he wasn't such a bad dude after all.")* Do you think Iggy did anything to help in the rescue of Max? Elaborate.

3. Why does Gwen remind Kevin that he has to be "extra careful"? *(Page 137, "She means the trouble he has sometimes catching his breath, because of the way his insides keep growing faster than his outside, which hasn't really grown at all.")*

4. Is school different for Freak the Mighty after Christmas vacation? *(Page 138, "The other thing about school that's different after Christmas vacation is how jealous everybody is that we got our pictures in the paper and on local TV.")* Do you think those who are jealous consider what Max and Kevin went through?

5. Does Max have to testify in court? *(Page 139, No. "What happened, they made a deal and Killer Kane pled guilty, which means he has to serve out the rest of his original sentence plus ten more years.")* Does this please Max? *(Page 139, "That should make me happy, but instead I feel really weird and worried...")*

6. What does Grim call Killer Kane? *(Page 139, Grim refers to Killer Kane as "an accident of nature.")* How does this worry Max? *(Page 139, "The weird thing I keep thinking about, what if something happens when I get older and I turn out to be another accident of nature?")*

7. What is "walking high"? *(Page 141, "Walking high" is what Max and Kevin call Max carrying Kevin around on his shoulders.)*

8. How does Kevin define *remembering*? *(Page 141, "Remembering is just an invention of the mind.")* What does Kevin mean by that? *(Page 142, "It means that if you want to, you can remember anything, whether it happened or not.")* Does that make sense to you? Why or why not? Explain.

9. What special birthday is Kevin celebrating a couple of days after school gets out? *(Page 143, Kevin is celebrating his thirteenth birthday.)* What else are Max and Kevin celebrating? *(Page 143, "The deal is, this is really two birthdays for the price of one, because Freak the Mighty is almost a year old.")*

10. What happens while Kevin is showing Grim how to play 3-D chess? *(Page 146, Kevin has a seizure.)*

Supplementary Activities:

1. Literary Analysis—Foreshadowing, continued: See # 3 of the Discussion Questions. Pages 143-144: With regard to Kevin's birthday gift, "What he's really getting, and I've been sworn to secrecy, is this new computer, the one he's been drooling over in his computer magazines. It comes with a modem, which means if he has to stay home for some reason, he can go to school over the telephone." Page 145: "...Freak asks me to flame out the candles (on his birthday cake) while he makes the wish, and then he doesn't even touch his piece, he just sort of pushes it around the plate. I figure he's...lost his appetite. Not that he's letting on he doesn't feel good...") What do you think the author has planned for Kevin?

2. What are the benefits and disadvantages of the Freak the Mighty combo? Make written lists. Summarize your lists and write a conclusion.

Freak the Mighty

Benefits	Disadvantages

Chapter 23: "The Empty Book"—Pages 147-152
Chapter 24: "The Return of Kicker"—Pages 153-157
Chapter 25: "What Loretta Said"—Pages 158-160

Summary:

After Kevin's first day in the hospital, Max walks there to be nearby. Max is allowed to see Kevin in the ICU. Kevin gives Max a book with blank pages and tells Max to write a book about the adventures of Freak the Mighty. When questioned by Max, Kevin tells him, "I'm not coming home. Not in my present manifestation." (page 149) Kevin tells Max that he will get the bionic body in the morning. Kevin has a coughing spell and the visit is cut short. Max walks to the hospital before daybreak the next morning. Max learns that Kevin has died. Max becomes hysterical and destroys some of the medical research area. Dr. Spivak listens as Max tells of Kevin's bionic dream. Max eventually writes the adventures of Freak the Mighty.

Vocabulary:

gyp 147   telemetry 148   tracheotomy 149
manifestation 149 stabilized 151

Discussion Questions:

1. What does Max take with him when he walks to the hospital to be near Kevin? *(Page 147, Max takes along the ornithopter.)* Why do you think he makes that choice?

2. Is Max allowed to see Kevin? Why or why not? *(Pages 148-149, Max is allowed to see Kevin in the ICU. As Dr. Spivak tells Max, "I thought no visitors was the best policy for now. But what Kevin wants, Kevin gets.")* Why do you think Dr. Spivak relented? Explain.

3. What does Kevin reply to Max's question as to when he is coming home from the hospital? *(Page 149, Kevin tells Max, "I'm not coming home. Not in my present manifestation." Page 150, "The next time you see me, I'll be new and improved.")* Do you think Max continues to believe Kevin? Why or why not?

4. What does Kevin want Max to do with the book of blank pages? *(Page 150, Kevin tells Max, "I want you to fill it up with our adventures.")* What is Kevin's excuse for not doing it? *(Page 151, "I won't have the time, so you'll have to do it.")* Does Max feel capable of fulfilling Kevin's request? Why or why not?

5. Why does Max's visit with Kevin end? *(Page 151, Kevin has a coughing spell.)* Is Kevin okay? *(Page 151, The ICU personnel stabilize Kevin.)* What do you think might have happened if Kevin had not been in the ICU?

6. Max leaves for the hospital before daybreak the next day. Why? *(Page 153, "The way I figure, I can check on Freak and be back in time for breakfast, no harm done.")* Why doesn't that happen? *(Pages 154-155, Kevin is already dead when Max arrives at the hospital.)*

7. How does Max react to the news of Kevin's death? *(Pages 155-157, Max gets hysterical, storms the Medical Research unit, is subdued by hospital guards, and tells Dr. Spivak of Kevin's dream of a bionic body.)* What does Dr. Spivak tell Max about Kevin? *(Page 157, "Kevin knew from a very young age that he wasn't going to have a very long life. He knew it was just a matter of time.")*

8. How does Dr. Spivak explain Kevin's fantasy to Max? *(Page 157, "I think he needed something to hope for and so he invented this rather remarkable fantasy you describe. Everybody needs something to hope for.")* How would you interpret Dr. Spivak's remarks?

---

9. What kind of reaction does Max have to Kevin's death? *(Page 158, "I don't know if this makes sense, but for a long time I felt like I was a balloon and somebody had let the air out of me. I didn't care if I ever got the air back, because what does it really matter if we're all going to die in the end?")* What do you think Kevin would say to Max, if he could? (See Supplementary Activities #2.)

10. Why does Max finally start to write the story of Freak the Mighty? *(Page 160, Max talks with Loretta Lee and tells her that he is doing "Nothing." Loretta Lee tells Max, "Nothing is a drag, kid. Think about it.")* Why do you think this comment gets Max started?

Supplementary Activities:
1. Invite a volunteer from an ICU to speak to the group. Have questions and comments prepared by the students.

2. Grim has two thoughts for Max: "…it isn't how long you've got that matters, it's what you do with the time you have…" and "Most of us go all the way through life and we never have a friend like Kevin. So maybe you should count yourself lucky." (pages 158-159) What is something different that Grim might have said to Max to convey the same messages?

3. Write the next chapter of the story.

4. Make and/or complete attribute webs for Kevin, Max, Gwen, Grim, Gram and Killer Kane.

5. Make a plot diagram for the story.

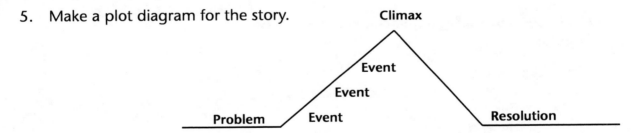

Postreading Questions

1. What do you think the lives of Max and Kevin might have been like had they not met one another again and become friends?

2. Why do you think Max and Kevin became such good friends? What did they do for one another?

3. What qualities do you think make a person a good friend? Make an attribute web for a good friend.

4. What are some of the things, over which Max and Kevin had no control, that influenced their lives greatly?

5. What do you think Max's life will be like from this time forward? (Will he be allowed to remain in the same classes? What kind of progress will he make?)

6. Theme (the novel's central idea)
   a) What is the author's message?
   b) Why do you think the author wrote this story?
   c) What do you think is the most important thing to remember about this story?Why?

7. Personal Opinion
   a) Which story character can you identify with the most? Why?
   b) What is your opinion of the ending of the novel?
   c) Do you feel that all of the issues raised by the author were resolved? Explain.
   d) Would you want to change something about this story? Elaborate.
   e) Would you recommend this novel to others? Why or why not?

8. Look at the illustration on the cover of the book. Has the cover artist depicted Max and Kevin as you have pictured them from the description in the story? Is there something you would change? Why or why not?

Postreading Extension Activities

Possible Areas of Study For Bulletin Board Projects:
Examples:

A. Friendship
   1. Definitions
      a. Friend
         A friend is a present you give yourself.
         A friend is someone who accepts you for who you are.
      b. Friendship
         Friendship is reliability.
         Friendship is courtesy.
   2. Attributes of a Good Friend
      A friend never judges.
      A friend lifts one's spirits.
   3. Value of Friendship
      Because of a friend, life is a little stronger, fuller and more gracious.

4. Poetry

    Livingston, Myra Cohn. *A Time to Talk: Poems of Friendship.* NY: McElderry Books, 1992.

    Hopkins, Lee. *Best Friends: Poems.* NY: Harper & Row, 1986.

5. Non-fiction Stories

    a. Real-life Friends

        Erlbach, Arlene. *The Best Friends Book: True Stories about Real Best Friends.* Minneapolis, MN: Free Spirit, '95

        Laskin, David. *A Common Life: Four Generations of American Literary Friendship and Influence.* NY: Simon & Schuster, 1994.

    b. Animal Friends

        King-Smith, Dick. *Dick King-Smith's Animal Friends: Thirty-one True Life Stories.* Cambridge, MA: Candlewick Press, 1996.

6. Death of a Friend

    Gootman, Marilyn. *When a Friend Dies: A Book for Teens about Grieving and Healing.* Minneapolis, MN: Free Spirit, 1994.

    Buckingham, Robert. *Coping with Grief.* NY: Rosen, 1991.

B. Robotics
1. Robot
   definition
   history
2. Automation
   definition
   history
   feedback
   computer use
3. Automation in Industry
4. Automation and Society
5. Automation and the Individual

C. Bionics—Bioengineering
1. Bionics
   definition
   applications
2. Bioengineering
   Biomechanical Engineering
   Biochemical Engineering
   Bioelectrical Engineering
3. Medical Implants

D. Physically and Mentally Challenged Individuals
1. Causes
2. Social Problems
3. Legal Rights

E. Additional Topics for Research
1. Arthurian Legend
2. Fireworks
3. Parole

Life:

Freak tells Max, page 53, that "Life is dangerous." How would you describe *life* in one or two words? Make a sample of a bumper sticker with a saying that begins with the words LIFE IS...

Grim:

Follow Max's suggestion on page 55, and "look under 'grim' in the dictionary..." Copy the definition of *grim* on a sheet of paper and list all of the synonyms and antonyms you can think of in a predetermined amount of time. Make a mini word search puzzle using as many of these words as possible.

Some Synonyms

stern	unyielding
forbidding	firm
fierce	inflexible
ferocious	implacable

Some Antonyms

amiable	smiling
inviting	reassuring
congenial	benign
pleasant	soft

F	I	G	N	I	R	U	S	S	A	E	R	F
I	I	P	L	E	A	S	A	N	T	T	O	S
N	C	E	I	Y	B	S	B	Q	F	R	T	H
F	O	F	R	M	H	A	O	O	B	E	G	G
L	N	E	P	C	P	N	S	I	R	V	N	N
E	G	L	Z	W	E	L	D	N	P	V	I	I
X	E	B	M	V	M	D	A	I	G	E	L	T
I	N	A	W	K	I	N	F	C	K	R	I	I
B	I	I	Y	N	G	H	H	I	A	F	M	V
L	A	M	G	I	O	V	W	I	R	B	S	N
E	L	A	N	F	G	N	Q	Z	A	M	L	I
N	G	E	F	E	R	O	C	I	O	U	S	E
P	B	Q	G	N	I	D	L	E	I	Y	N	U

WORD LIST

AMIABLE	INFLEXIBLE
BENIGN	INVITING
CONGENIAL	PLEASANT
FEROCIOUS	REASSURING
FIERCE	SMILING
FIRM	SOFT
FORBIDDING	STERN
IMPLACABLE	UNYIELDING

New Testaments:

Freak the Mighty's quest for treasure leads to the New Tenements apartment buildings, called the New Testaments by the local population. Place the letters of New Testaments in a vertical line on a sheet of paper. Use each letter as the first letter of a word that you think relates to Freak the Mighty (Max + Kevin). For example:

Nickname
Effective
Watchful

Tenacious
Eager
Sagacious
Transformed
Ardent
Mindful
Earnest
Necessary
Temporary
Serious

Use as many of the words as possible in a written description of Freak the Mighty.

Place the letters of Freak the Mighty in a line. How many words can you make from the letters, other than freak/the/mighty, in five minutes?

Example of some of the words:

FREAKTHEMIGHTY

3-letter words	4-letter words			5-letter words	6-letter words	7-letter words
rim	trim	meat	mite	right	fright	heather
him	free	heat	reef	three	height	fighter
kit	tree	mitt	fret	there	hearty	
hit	year	meet	raft	tight	hearth	
hem	tear	mare	hear	great	heater	
yet	them	hike	kite	greet	meager	

Pyramid:
Kevin makes a pyramid to house Max's Christmas gift. (page 96)

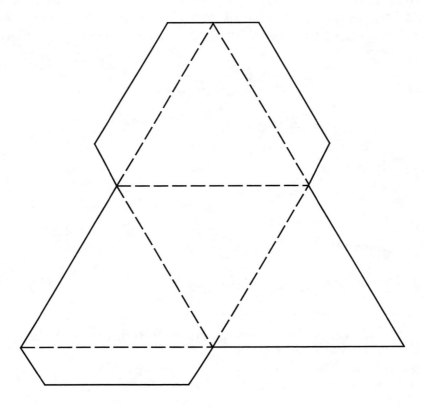

Directions: To make the pyramid, cut out on the solid lines. Fold along broken lines. Use tabs for gluing.

This is a pyramid that is made up of four triangles whose sides are the same length.

1) What is the name of the triangle whose sides are equal?_____

2) What is the perimeter of one triangle if one of its sides is equal to :

   a. 3 inches   _____

   b. 36 centimeters _____

   c. 1-1/2 feet   _____

3) What is the surface area of the pyramid if the surface area of one triangle is

   9 square inches?   _____

Vocabulary Word Search Puzzle

Directions: Do the word search. Find the words that may be printed forwards, backwards, horizontally, vertically, and on a diagonal. Write down the letters that have not been used, starting at the top and working left to right in each row. Group the letters into words to find the hidden message.

T	H	T	B	E	D	T	O	C	I	X	E	L	S	Y	D	E	D	D	D
P	R	U	C	U	V	I	R	E	D	E	E	M	E	D	T	U	E	E	D
N	R	A	N	A	L	A	M	G	L	E	U	R	G	A	P	T	Z	E	I
A	A	O	J	K	F	K	S	A	E	P	Y	G	I	L	E	I	T	M	T
P	C	N	P	E	E	I	H	I	R	H	E	P	E	N	L	A	P	T	M
S	U	C	O	U	C	R	T	E	V	Y	O	X	T	I	L	R	E	E	R
T	P	N	E	S	L	T	I	R	A	E	P	I	B	U	E	L	G	M	R
N	A	A	K	L	E	S	O	N	A	D	O	A	T	S	E	A	V	X	E
E	N	G	S	S	E	C	I	R	G	N	T	S	S	P	P	A	E	D	T
M	O	I	T	T	R	O	O	Y	S	O	I	O	H	N	S	G	I	P	
E	I	Z	S	D	I	E	A	N	N	P	O	R	O	Y	F	H	E	O	O
C	S	M	E	R	E	C	R	T	D	N	T	N	R	D	A	T	T	N	H
A	I	O	U	K	H	E	C	S	O	A	E	T	E	D	W	A	A	A	T
L	C	E	Q	U	L	I	P	C	T	R	E	P	S	E	A	O	T	M	I
P	N	R	F	T	N	R	L	I	N	M	R	Y	L	C	R	M	E	U	N
E	I	F	T	E	O	U	O	I	E	I	E	U	O	I	I	B	S	H	R
R	E	U	G	D	N	N	T	L	V	N	B	E	A	N	N	N	M	E	O
D	C	O	I	K	T	E	E	E	A	R	E	S	A	L	D	E	O	O	L
S	I	G	E	B	R	T	D	R	O	B	O	T	I	C	S	E	A	I	H
B	Y	R	L	C	M	I	C	R	O	S	E	C	O	N	D	E	R	R	B

TELEMETRY	DYSLEXIC	BIONICS	DEPRIVED
YONDER	EVASIVE	REPLACEMENT	TELEPORTATION
LASER	SPASTIC	HUNKERING	MICROSECOND
HUFFED	CRETIN	INCISION	PUNKSTERS
DETENTION	GIZMO	IMPRESSION	PYRAMID
ACCELERATOR	ORNITHOPTER	LINEAR	QUEST
BIOGENIC	GRUEL	NANOSECOND	REDEEMED
POSTULATED	ARTIFACT	OATHS	ROBOTICS
BULKHEAD	GYP	OPIATE	STABILIZED
CLUNKER	SCUTTLE	PRODIGY	TRAJECTORY
HUMANOID	HOMBRE	VEGETATE	MEGAPHONE
DUPLEX	DAMSEL	PROPULSION	

Some other things to do:

1. Put the words in alphabetical order.

2. Number the words and define every odd-numbered word and use every even-numbered word in a sentence.

Vocabulary Crossword Puzzle

Directions: Use the clues to figure out the answers to the crossword puzzle.

Across

3 consumed	14 conflict	24 restraints
4 fellow	18 discharge	26 advanced
8 guessed	19 trespassing	
12 results	23 made known	

Down

1 brief look
2 view
5 best
6 mission
7 typical example
9 scrutiny
10 manner
11 small
13 fake
15 insulted
16 wince
17 indestructible
20 delicate
21 thin porridge
22 gadget
25 complacent

Words Used

confrontation	quest	observation
sophisticated	flinch	offended
consequences	flimsy	invincible
glimpse	postulated	optimum
phony	expel	gizmo
hombre	divulged	archetype
demeanor	limitations	gruel
intruding	perspective	smug
puny	depleted	

Bibliography

Berger, Fredericka. *Robots: What They Are, What They Do.* NY: Greenwillow Books, 1992.

Cummings, Rhoda. *The School Survival Guide for Kids with LD.* Minneapolis, MN: Free Spirit Publishers, 1991.

Darling, David. *Computers of the Future.* Parsippany, NJ: Dillon Press, 1996.

Dwyer, Kathleen. *What Do You Mean I Have a Learning Disability?* NY: Walker & Company, 1991.

Gehret, Jeanne. *The Don't-give-up Kid and Learning Differences.* Fairport, NY: Verbal Images Press, 1990.

Hall, David. *Living with Learning Disabilities: A Guide for Students.* Minneapolis, MN: Lerner Publications, 1993.

Harrar, George. *Radical Robots: Can You Be Replaced?* NY: Simon & Schuster, 1990.

Harris, Jacqueline. *Learning Disorders.* NY: Twenty-first Century Books, 1993.

Landau, Elaine. *Dyslexia.* NY: F. Watts, 1991.

Metos, Thomas. *Artificial Humans: Transplants and Bionics.* NY: Messner, 1985.

Roby, Cynthia. *When Learning Is Tough: Kids Talk about Their Learning Disabilities.* Morton Grove, IL: A. Whitman & Company, 1994.

Skurzynski, Gloria. *Robots: Your High-Tech World.* NY: Bradbury Press, 1990.

Resources (This 1997 information is subject to change without notice.)

Canadian Society for Mucopolysaccharaide and Related Diseases, Inc., 204-4912 Ross Street, Red Deer, Alberta T4N 1X7, Canada

March of Dimes Birth Defects Foundation 1, 275 Mamaroneck Avenue, White Plains, NY 10605

National MPS (Mucopolysaccharidoses/Mucolipidoses) Society, 17 Kraemer Street, Hicksville, NY 11801

NIH/National Digestive Diseases Information Clearinghouse Two, Information Way, Bethesda, MD 20892-3570

Research Trust for Metabolic Diseases in Children, Golden Gates Lodge, Weston Road, Crewe CWI IXN United Kingdom

Society of Mucopolysaccharaide (MPS) Disease, United Kingdom, 7 Chessfield Park, Buckinghamshire HP6 6RU, United Kingdom

Vaincre Les Maladies Lysosomales, 9 Place du 19 Mars 1962, 91035, Evry Cedex, France

Assessment for *Freak the Mighty* by Rodman Philbrick

Assessment is an on-going process. The following ten items can be completed during the novel study. When an item is completed, the student places the date of completion on the line that is next to it under the STUDENT column. When the teacher and the student check the item together, the date is placed on the line that is next to it under the TEACHER column.

Name _____

Student   **Teacher**

_____   _____   1. How does Grim differentiate between a lie and a tale? Explain.

_____   _____   2. What is *parole*? How does it relate to the story?

_____   _____   3. What is the immediate benefit Kevin and Max each get when they become Freak the Mighty?

_____   _____   4. Why does Max live with his grandparents, Gram and Grim? Elaborate.

_____   _____   5. Why does Kevin's body remain small? Do Kevin's internal organs grow? What is the result of this?

_____   _____   6. What is Kevin's dream of replacement parts for his body? Do you think this is realistic?

_____   _____   7. Who are Loretta and Iggy Lee? What parts do they play in this story?

_____   _____   8. What happens to Max on Christmas Eve? Who helps Max? Elaborate.

_____   _____   9. What happens to Kevin on his birthday? What is the outcome?

_____   _____   10. Complete three of the vocabulary activities.

Answer Sheet

Assessment (answers should include some of the following):

1. Grim believes that "Lies are mean things, and tales are meant to entertain." (page 95)
2. Parole, in criminal law, is a pledge of good conduct given by a person convicted of a crime as a condition of release from imprisonment before the expiration of the term of confinement. Killer Kane is granted parole and kidnaps Max.
3. They both get a friend and companionship. Kevin gets the use of Max's long legs and transportation. Max gets the use of Kevin's creativity, self-determination and intelligence.
4. Max lives with his grandparents because Max's father is in prison for killing Max's mother.
5. Kevin has a birth defect. His body does not grow, but his internal organs do. This results in continued pressure on the organs and ultimately early death.
6. Kevin dreams that he will be given a replacement body.
7. Loretta and Iggy Lee are members of a motorcycle gang and live in an apartment in the New Testaments. They know Killer Kane. They help Max when he is kidnapped.
8. Max is kidnapped, and almost killed, by his father on Christmas Eve. Loretta and Iggy help Max.
9. Kevin has a seizure on his birthday. He is hospitalized and dies.
10. student generated

Pyramid:

1. equilateral triangle
2. a. perimeter if one side is 3 inches   9 inches
   b. perimeter if one side is 36 centimeters   108 centimeters
   c. perimeter if one side is 1-1/2 feet   4-1/2 feet
3. surface area   36 square inches

Grim Mini Word Search Puzzle:

Puzzle Answers

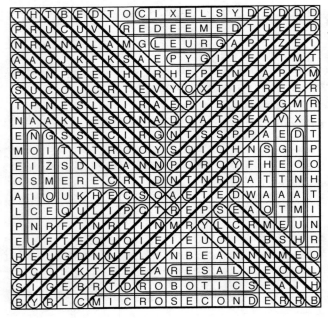

Hidden Message:
TOGETHER MAX AND FREAK WERE UNBEATABLE

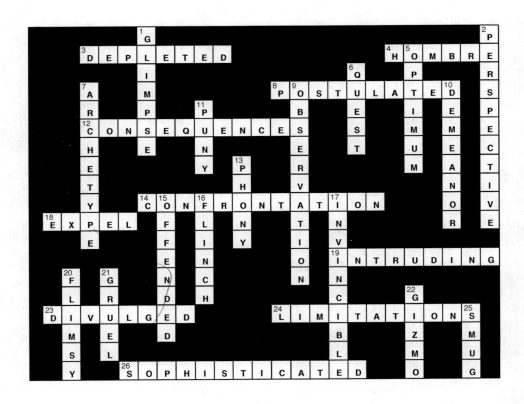